United States Government Accountability Office

GAO

Report to the Chairman, Subcommittee on Livestock, Dairy, Poultry, Marketing and Agriculture Security, Committee on Agriculture, Nutrition, and Forestry, U.S. Senate

September 2012

H-2A VISA PROGRAM

Modernization and Improved Guidance Could Reduce Employer Application Burden

G A O
Accountability ★ Integrity ★ Reliability

GAO-12-706

September 2012

GAO
Accountability * Integrity * Reliability

Highlights

Highlights of GAO-12-706, a report to the Chairman, Subcommittee on Livestock, Dairy, Poultry, Marketing and Agriculture Security, Committee on Agriculture, Nutrition, and Forestry, U.S. Senate

H-2A VISA PROGRAM

Modernization and Improved Guidance Could Reduce Employer Application Burden

Why GAO Did This Study

The H-2A visa program allows U.S. employers anticipating a shortage of domestic agricultural workers to hire foreign workers on a temporary basis. State workforce agencies and three federal agencies—the Departments of Labor, Homeland Security, and State review applications for such workers. GAO was asked to examine (1) any aspects of the application process that present challenges to agricultural employers, and (2) how federal agencies have addressed any employer challenges with the application process. GAO analyzed Labor and DHS data; interviewed agency officials and employer representatives; and conducted site visits in New York, North Carolina, and Washington.

What GAO Recommends

GAO recommends that (1) Labor and DHS use their new electronic application systems to collect data on reasons applications are delayed and use this information to improve the timeliness of application processing; (2) Labor allow employers to submit one application for groups of similar workers needed in a single season; and (3) Labor review and revise, as appropriate, its guidance to states regarding methods for determining the acceptability of employment practices in employers' applications. DHS and Labor agreed with the recommendation to collect additional data and Labor agreed with the recommendation to update its guidance. Labor disagreed with the recommendation it allow employers to apply once per season. GAO believes the recommendation is still valid and that a single application does not preclude timely testing of the labor market as workers are needed.

View GAO-12-706. For more information, contact Revae Moran at (202) 512-7215 or moranr@gao.gov

What GAO Found

Over 90 percent of employer applications for H-2A workers were approved in fiscal year (FY) 2011, but some employers experienced processing delays. For example, the Department of Labor (Labor) processed 63 percent of applications in a timely manner in FY 2011, but 37 percent were processed after the deadline, including 7 percent that were approved less than 15 days before workers were needed. This left some employers little time for the second phase of the application process, which is managed by the Department of Homeland Security (DHS), and for workers to obtain visas from the Department of State (State). Although workers can apply for visas online, most of the H-2A process involves paper handling, which contributes to processing delays. In addition, employers who need workers at different times of the season must repeat the entire process for each group of workers. Although the agencies lack data on the reasons for processing delays, employers reported delays due to increased scrutiny by Labor and DHS when these agencies implemented new rules and procedures intended to improve program integrity and protect workers. For example, in FY 2011, Labor notified 63 percent of employers that their applications required changes or additional documentation to comply with its new rules, up sharply from previous years.

Percentage of Employer Applications Requiring Changes or Additional Documentation (FY 2006-2011)

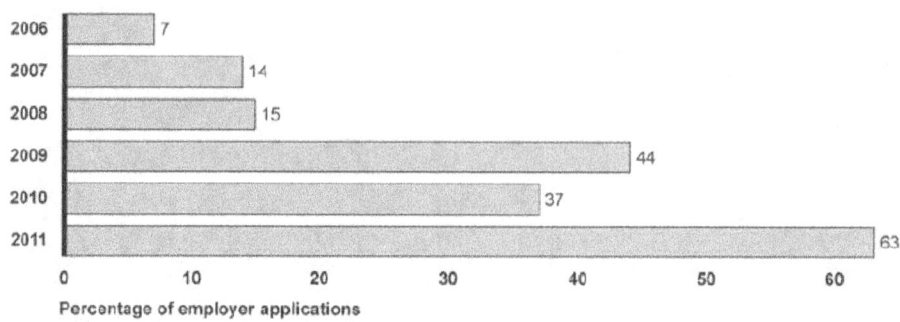

Percentage of employer applications

Year	Percentage
2006	7
2007	14
2008	15
2009	44
2010	37
2011	63

Source: GAO analysis of Department of Labor data.

Federal agencies are taking steps to improve the H-2A application process. Labor and DHS are developing new electronic application systems, but both agencies' systems have been delayed. Labor also recently began using e-mail to resolve issues with employers, and all three agencies provided more information to employers to clarify program requirements. Even with these efforts, some employers view Labor's decisions as inconsistent. For example, some employers received different decisions about issues such as whether they can require workers to have experience in farm work and questioned the methods states used to decide whether the job qualifications in their applications were acceptable. We found states used different methods to determine acceptable qualifications, which is allowed under Labor's guidance.

_____ **United States Government Accountability Office**

Contents

Abbreviations

DHS	Department of Homeland Security
INA	Immigration and Nationality Act
Labor	Department of Labor
State	Department of State

United States Government Accountability Office
Washington, DC 20548

September 12, 2012

The Honorable Kirsten Gillibrand
Chairman
Subcommittee on Livestock, Dairy, Poultry, Marketing
    and Agriculture Security
Committee on Agriculture, Nutrition, and Forestry
United States Senate

Dear Madam Chairman:

The nation's agricultural sector relies on hired farm workers to bring products to market. Obtaining enough workers at the right time is critical, especially for producers of crops with short harvest seasons. Because it is difficult for some agricultural employers to find enough U.S. workers, federal law allows these employers to apply for permission to hire foreign workers on a temporary or seasonal basis and arrange for their entry into the country under special visas, known as H-2A visas.[1] About 55,000 H-2A visas were issued in fiscal year 2011, according to the Department of State (State). To ensure protections for workers and proper vetting of these foreign workers before entry, state workforce agencies and three federal agencies are involved in administering the H-2A process—the Departments of Labor (Labor), Homeland Security (DHS), and State. Before employers can employ H-2A workers, they must apply for a certification from Labor that a labor shortage exists in their particular case and U.S. workers will not be adversely affected by hiring H-2A workers. If Labor determines these conditions are met, an employer can submit a petition to DHS to employ foreign workers. If DHS approves the petition, foreign workers can apply to State for a H-2A visa. In 1997, we reviewed the H-2A program and made recommendations to improve service to employers and reduce the amount of time it takes federal agencies to process employer applications for H-2A workers.[2] Agencies have implemented some of our recommendations, but questions about whether

---

[1] 8 U.S.C. §§ 1101(a)(15)(H)(ii)(a) and 1188.

[2] GAO, GAO- H-2A *Agricultural Guestworker Program: Changes Could Improve Services to Employers and Better Protect Workers*, GAO/HEHS-98-20 (Washington, D.C.: Dec. 31, 1997). GAO, GAO- H-2A *Agricultural Guestworkers: Status of Efforts to Improve Program Services*, GAO/T-HEHS-00-134 (Washington, D.C.: June 15, 2000).

GAO-12-706 H-2A Application Process

the H-2A program meets employers' needs were raised in recent congressional hearings. In response to your request, to identify ways to expedite the application process while maintaining worker protections and national security, we examined (1) what aspects of the application process, if any, present challenges to agricultural employers, and (2) how federal agencies have addressed any employer challenges with the application process.

To identify potential challenges employers experience when applying for H-2A workers, we interviewed representatives from 25 employers and 12 agricultural employer associations. We identified these employers through national employer associations and regional associations in the states we visited. We also visited three states (New York, North Carolina, and Washington), which we selected because they account for a sizable proportion of all H-2A workers (about 24 percent of H-2A positions certified in fiscal year 2011 according to data reported by Labor) and vary in geographic location. Within each state, we interviewed a combination of state workforce agency officials, representatives from agricultural employer associations, employers, and farm worker advocates. Information obtained from our site visits and employer interviews cannot be generalized to all states or agricultural employers. To review the timeliness of application processing, we analyzed data from Labor for fiscal years 2006 through 2012 and from DHS for fiscal years 2006 through 2011. To assess the reliability of the data, we reviewed agency documentation, interviewed Labor and DHS officials, tested the electronic data, and compared our results with related information reported by the agencies. Based on these reviews, we determined that the data used to determine the timeliness of application processing were sufficiently reliable for the purposes of this report. We reviewed Labor's data on the number of H-2A workers employers requested and the number of H-2A workers certified by Labor, and determined that these data were not sufficiently reliable for our purposes. As a result, we did not report the total number of H-2A workers requested and certified. We will issue a separate management letter to Labor detailing our findings related to this information. We also reviewed employer appeals of Labor's adverse rulings to identify the reasons for the appeals and the extent to which

Labor's decisions were affirmed or reversed.[3] To identify actions taken by the agencies to address employer challenges, we interviewed federal officials who process H-2A applications at Labor, DHS, and State. We also reviewed agency procedures, relevant federal laws and regulations, and some recent legislative proposals to modify or replace the H-2A program. We conducted this performance audit from October 2011 to September 2012 in accordance with generally accepted government auditing standards. Those standards require that we plan and perform the audit to obtain sufficient, appropriate evidence to provide a reasonable basis for our findings and conclusions based on our audit objectives. We believe that the evidence obtained provides a reasonable basis for our findings and conclusions based on our audit objectives.

Background

Origin of the H-2A Program

The H-2A program was preceded by several other temporary worker programs designed to address farm labor shortages in the United States. During World War I, the Congress authorized the issuance of rules providing for the temporary admission of otherwise inadmissible aliens, and this led to the establishment of a temporary farm labor program designed to replace U.S. workers directly involved in the war effort.[4] Similarly, initially through an agreement with Mexico, a guest worker program was authorized during World War II that brought in over 4 million Mexican workers from 1942 to 1964, called "braceros" to work on farms on a seasonal basis.[5] Although the Bracero program expanded the farm labor supply, the program also affected domestic farm workers through reduced wages and employment, according to a 2009 Congressional

---

[3]Such decisions include Labor's decisions to send the employer a deficiency notice requesting additional documentation or corrections to an employer's application package or Labor's denial of an employer's request for permission to hire foreign workers under the H-2A program. Employers may appeal Labor's deficiency notices or denials to an Administrative Law judge within Labor's Office of Administrative Law Judges. This judge may affirm, reverse, or modify Labor's decision; remand the case back to Labor for further action; or dismiss the case.

[4]Act of February 5, 1917, ch. 29, § 3, 39 Stat. 874, 875-78.

[5]Agreement Between the United States of America and Mexico Respecting the Temporary Migration of Mexican Agricultural Workers, U.S.-Mex., Aug. 4, 1942, 1942 U.S.T. 209.

GAO-12-706 H-2A Application Process

Research Service report.[6] The Bracero program has been criticized by labor groups, which identified issues such as mistreatment of workers and lax enforcement of work contracts. While the Bracero program was still in effect, the Immigration and Nationality Act of 1952 (INA) established the statutory authority for a guestworker program that included workers performing temporary services or labor, known as "H-2" after the specific provision of the law.[7] The Immigration Reform and Control Act of 1986 amended the INA and effectively divided the H-2 program into two programs: the H-2A program expressly for agricultural employers and the H-2B program expressly for nonagricultural employers.[8]

The H-2A program was created to help agricultural employers obtain an adequate labor supply while also protecting the jobs, wages, and working conditions of U.S. farm workers.[9] The H-2A law and regulations contain several requirements to protect U.S. workers from adverse effects associated with the hiring of temporary foreign workers and to protect foreign workers from exploitation.[10] Under the program, employers must provide H-2A workers a minimum level of wages, benefits, and working conditions. For example, employers must pay a prescribed wage rate, provide the workers housing that meets minimum standards for health and safety, pay for workers' travel costs to and from their home country, and guarantee workers will be paid for three-quarters of the work contract even if less work is needed.[11] (see table 1 for more information about the conditions of employment that employers are expected to provide workers).

---

[6]Congressional Research Service, *The Effects on U.S. Farm Workers of an Agricultural Guest Worker Program.* Linda Levine, Specialist in Labor Economics, (Washington, D.C.: Dec. 28, 2009).

[7]Pub. L. No. 82-414, § 101(a)(15)(H)(ii), 66 Stat. 163, 169 (codified as amended at 8 U.S.C. § 1101(a)(15)(H)(ii)(A) and (B)). INA bars the admission of a foreign worker who seeks to enter the United States under a H-2A visa, unless the Secretary of Labor provides a certification to the Secretaries of State and DHS.

[8]Pub. L. No. 99-603, § 301(a), 100 Stat. 3359, 3411 (codified as amended at 8 U.S.C. § 1101(a)(15)(H)(ii)(A)).

[9]H.R. Rpt. 99-682, pt. 1, at 79 (1986).

[10]8 U.S.C. §§ 1101(a)(15)(H)(ii)(A) and 1188, and 20 C.F.R. pt. 655, subpt. B (2012).

[11]20 U.S.C. § 655.122(c), (d), (h), (i) and (l) (2012).

Table 1: Key Department of Labor H-2A Program Requirements

Issue	Requirements
Recruitment of U.S. Workers	• Demonstrate need for a specific number of H-2A workers by completing specific U.S. recruitment activities coordinated through the state workforce agency. • Contact certain former employees and engage in positive recruitment of U.S. workers. • Hire any qualified, eligible U.S. worker until half of the contract work period is over (known as 50 percent rule) and only reject U.S. workers for lawful, job-related reasons.[a] • Offer U.S. workers terms and working conditions not less favorable than those offered to H-2A workers.
Rates of Pay	Pay all covered workers (H-2A and U.S. workers in corresponding employment) at least the highest of various wage rates specified in regulation. Wages may be calculated on the basis of hourly or "piece" rates of pay.
Recordkeeping	Employers must keep accurate records of hours of work offered and hours actually worked each day. On or before each payday (which must be at least twice monthly), each worker must be given an hours and earnings statement showing hours offered, hours actually worked, hourly rate and/or piece rate of pay, and if piece rates are used, units produced daily. The statement must also indicate total earnings for the pay period and all deductions from wages.
Written Disclosure of the Work Contract	Provide each worker a copy of the work contract—in a language understood by the worker—that describes the terms and conditions of employment, or in the absence of a written work contract, a copy of the job order submitted and approved by the department.
Guarantees to All Workers	Guarantee to offer to each covered worker employment for a total number of hours equal to at least 75% of the workdays in the contract period—called the "three-fourths guarantee."
Housing and Meals	• Provide housing, which meets all applicable safety standards, at no cost to H-2A workers and to workers in corresponding employment who are not reasonably able to return to their residence within the same day. • Provide each covered worker with three meals per day or furnish free and convenient cooking and kitchen facilities where workers can prepare their own meals.
Transportation	Provide daily transportation between the workers' living quarters and the employer's worksite at no cost to covered workers living in employer-provided housing. Employer-provided transportation must meet all applicable safety standards, be properly insured, and be operated by licensed drivers.
Inbound & Outbound Expenses	If not previously advanced or otherwise provided, the employer must reimburse workers for reasonable costs incurred for inbound transportation and subsistence costs once the worker completes 50% of the work contract period and outbound transportation and subsistence costs upon completion of the work contract.
Prohibitions Against Confiscating Workers' Documents and Charging Certain Fees	• Comply with all applicable laws and regulations, including the prohibition against holding or confiscating workers' passports or other immigration documents. • Employers must not seek or receive payment of any kind from workers for anything related to obtaining the H-2A labor certification, including the employer's attorney or agent fees, application fees, or recruitment costs.
Notification of Worker Abandonment or Termination	Notify Labor in writing within 2 workdays if any worker (H-2A or U.S. worker) voluntarily abandons the job or is terminated for cause before the end of the certified work period. The employer also must notify DHS within 2 workdays if an H-2A worker abandons or is terminated from the job.

Source: Department of Labor H-2A Compliance Fact Sheets.

[a]Employers applying individually (not part of a joint application) who did not use more than 500 days of agricultural labor in any quarter during the preceding calendar year are exempt from the 50 percent rule. 20 C.F.R. § 655.135(d) (2012).

Current Use of the H-2A Program

In fiscal year 2011, Labor received about 4,900 employer applications requesting permission to hire H-2A workers.[12] State issued about 55,000 H-2A visas in fiscal year 2011 and about 94 percent of these visas were processed by Mexican posts, according to data reported by State. Employers requested H-2A workers to help support the production of various commodities, such as fruit, vegetables, tobacco, and grain. While many of these employers requested help with general farm work, others sought workers with special skills, such as sheepherders or combine operators. Employers in some states rely more heavily on H-2A workers to meet their labor needs. In fiscal year 2011, Labor reported that over half of the H-2A positions it certified were located in five southeastern states—North Carolina, Florida, Georgia, Louisiana, and Kentucky.[13] Although California is the largest producer of agricultural products in the country, the state is ranked thirteenth in its employment of H-2A workers, according to a recent Labor report. H-2A workers are expected to work temporarily and must leave the country once the temporary work contract is complete, but may return in future years to meet employers' seasonal needs under specific circumstances.[14] In fiscal year 2011, about 27 percent of H-2A employers requested H-2A workers for 6 months or less and about 73 percent of employers requested workers for 7 to 12 months.

H-2A workers represent a small proportion of the approximately 1 million hired agricultural workers that the U.S. Department of Agriculture estimates are in the United States, many of whom are not legally authorized to work in the country (referred to as undocumented workers). Research suggests that about half of all U.S. agricultural workers are undocumented.[15] An employer may inadvertently hire undocumented

---

[12]Employers can request multiple H-2A workers on one application. H-2A employers represent a small proportion of the approximately 2.2 million U.S. farms in fiscal year 2010, according to estimates reported by the U.S. Department of Agriculture.

[13]The top 10 states in the number of positions approved by Labor under the H-2A program in fiscal year 2011 were North Carolina, Florida, Georgia, Louisiana, Kentucky, Arizona, New York, Washington, Virginia, and South Carolina.

[14]20 C.F.R. § 655.135(i) (2011). For qualifying work, workers may get extensions up to a maximum total stay of 3 years and then, after being out of the United States for at least 3 months, apply for readmission in future years for additional qualifying work. 8 C.F.R. § 214.2(h)(5)(viii)(C) (2012).

[15]The U.S. Department of Agriculture's Economic Research Service analyzed Labor's National Agricultural Workers Survey data and found that, on average, the proportion of hired crop farm workers who were not legally authorized to work in the United States from 2007 to 2009 was around 50 percent.

workers if the workers give the employer fraudulent documents. Employers may also choose to violate the law and knowingly hire undocumented workers rather than employing U.S. workers or participating in the H-2A program and meeting its associated requirements.[16] However, employers knowingly hiring undocumented workers rather than using the legal H-2A process risk penalties or workforce disruption through DHS's enforcement of immigration law or from state actions that may affect the availability of undocumented workers.

Overview of the H-2A Application Process

To request H-2A workers, employers apply consecutively to their state workforce agency,[17] Labor, and DHS; and prospective workers apply to State for H-2A visas. Under the law and Labor's H-2A regulations, state workforce agencies, Labor, and employers are subject to specific deadlines for processing H-2A applications (see fig. 1).[18] DHS and State are not subject to processing deadlines under relevant statutes and regulations, according to agency officials.

---

[16]To limit liability should employers inadvertently hire undocumented workers, employers may follow statutorily prescribed procedures for verifying that an individual is legally authorized to work in the United States. 8 U.S.C. § 1324a(a)(3) and (b).

[17]State workforce agencies oversee and provide employment and workforce development services. Employers who need workers in more than one state within the same geographic area may submit applications for H-2A workers to any one of the state workforce agencies covering the anticipated locations. 20 C.F.R. § 655.121(a)(1) (2012).

[18]8 U.S.C. § 1188(c) and 20 C.F.R. §§ 121(a), 655.130 - 655.133, 655.140 - 655.143, and 655.160. Prior to 1999, Labor had more time to review employer applications. Congress amended the INA in 1999 to allow employers to submit applications to Labor later and require Labor to make certification decisions earlier, effectively compressing the minimum time available for Labor to process applications from 40 days to 15. Agriculture, Rural Development, Food and Drug Administration, and Related Agencies Appropriations Act, 2000, Pub. L. No. 106-78, § 748,113 Stat. 1135, 1167(codified at 8 U.S.C. § 1188(c)(3)) (1999). Specifically, the 1999 act changed the requirement that employers file applications from at least 60 days before the first date the employer needs workers to at least 45 days before the date of need. Labor was then required to issue certification decisions no later than 30 days before the employer's date of need rather than 20 days before the date of need.

Figure 1: Deadlines for Applying for Workers under the H-2A Program

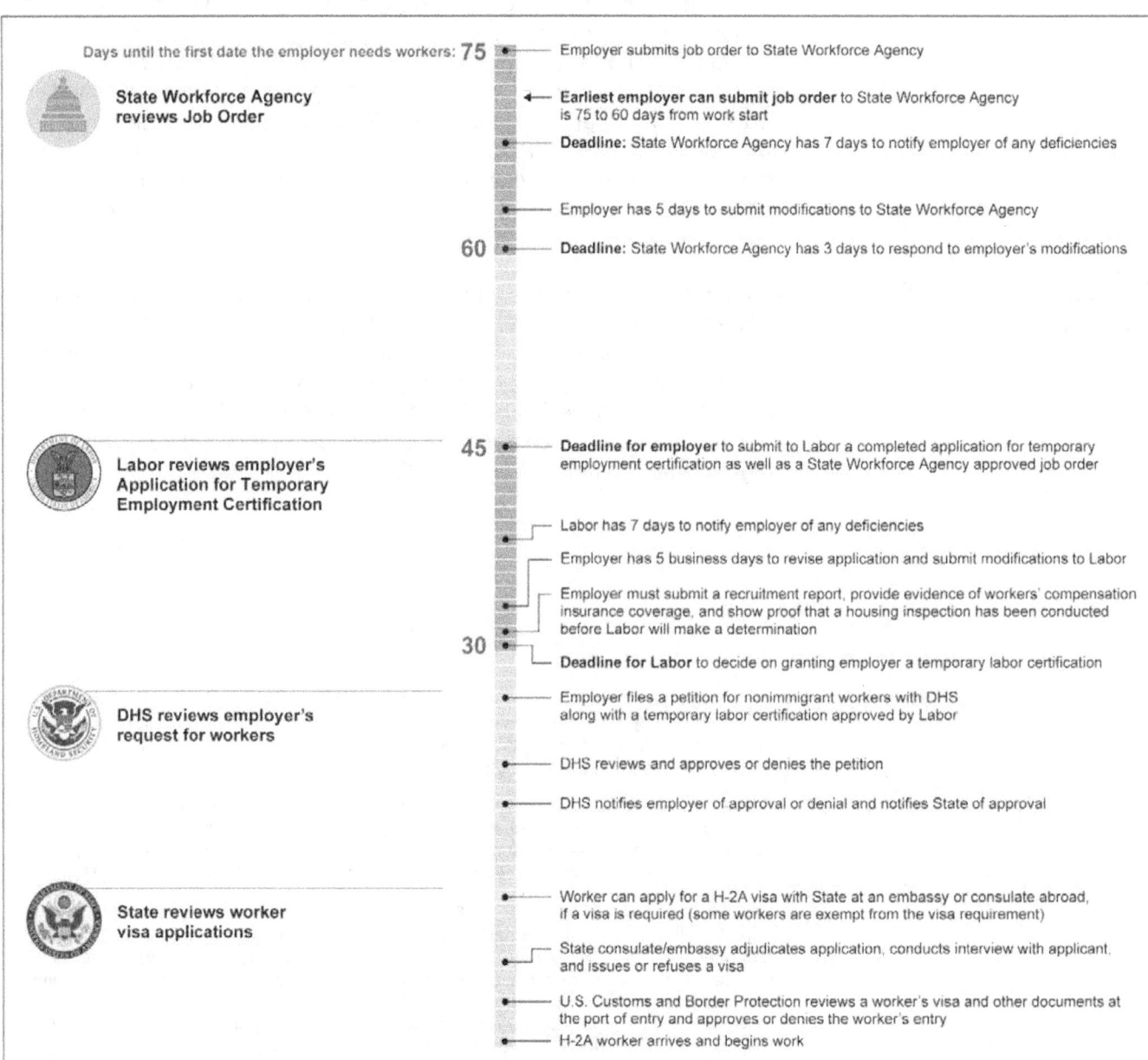

Source: GAO analysis of Labor and DHS regulations and guidance.

Employers interested in hiring H-2A workers must seek approval of the proposed terms and conditions of employment from their state workforce agencies and submit application packages to Labor.[19] First, employers must submit job orders to their state workforce agencies describing the jobs they are seeking to fill and the number of workers needed. The state workforce agencies review the job orders for compliance with Labor's H-2A regulations and may provide employers information about the wages and employment practices that apply in their states.[20] During their review, state workforce agencies may ask employers to make corrections or provide additional documentation. Upon approval, the state workforce agencies begin assisting employers in trying to recruit U.S. workers. Employers must conduct various recruitment activities and accept referrals of all eligible U.S. workers that apply for the jobs until the date on which the H-2A workers depart for the place of work.

Following approval of their job orders by the state workforce agencies, employers apply for temporary employment certifications from Labor by submitting the job orders, applications, and appendices signed by the employers stating that they are in compliance with and will continue to comply with all applicable federal requirements.[21] If an application is incomplete or incorrect, Labor may send the employer a notice of deficiency asking for additional documentation or corrections. After the employer provides the additional information or makes the needed corrections and Labor determines the application and job order are complete and meet all requirements, it will send a notice of acceptance and direct the employer to complete specific recruitment activities and submit additional documentation, such as a report describing the employer's efforts to recruit U.S. workers. Labor is to then grant the employer a temporary labor certification if the employer has established the need for the agricultural service or labor to be performed on a temporary or seasonal basis and complied with all the procedural requirements as well as all applicable regulatory requirements imposed to

---

[19]20 C.F.R. pt. 655, subpt. B (2012).

[20]States develop and carry out surveys of employers and use other data collection methods to determine wages and employment standards in their state.

[21]The regulation refers to the job order as a Form ETA-790. Applications for temporary employment certification may be filed by an individual employer, an agent working for the employer (e.g., lawyer or labor contractor), or by an employer association on behalf of multiple employers.

ascertain that (1) there are not sufficient U.S. workers who are qualified and available to perform the work, and (2) employing foreign workers will not adversely affect the wages and working conditions of similarly employed U.S. workers.[22]

After receiving temporary employment certifications from Labor, employers submit petitions to DHS requesting that a specific number of individuals be classified as H-2A workers for the certified job openings.[23] The petition includes Labor's certification, information about the employer, the positions the H-2A workers will fill, and the workers' names, if listed by the employer.[24] If questions arise, DHS may send the employer a request for additional documentation.

Following approval of the employer's petition by DHS, prospective workers can apply with State for H-2A visas, if a visa is required.[25] State operates visa-issuing posts abroad.[26] Employers may work with foreign labor contractors who help them recruit workers and help workers with the visa application process. State's process for determining who will be issued or refused a visa contains several steps, including reviewing visa applications, checking databases to identify issues, such as security concerns, collecting potential workers' fingerprints and photos, and conducting in-person interviews of workers. State may deny a visa based on certain criminal and related grounds, security and related grounds, or

---

[22]8 U.S.C. § 1188(a) and 20 C.F.R. § 655.161 (2012).

[23]8 C.F.R. § 214.2(h)(5) (2012).

[24]Employers are required to provide the names of the workers if they are requesting to extend a worker's length of stay or if the worker comes from a country that is not on DHS's list of countries from which H-2A workers may be requested. Naming specific workers on the application to DHS is otherwise voluntary. 8 C.F.R. § 214.2(h)(2)(iiii) (2012). When workers' names are identified in the applications, DHS checks these names against databases to identify issues, such as criminal histories, that may prevent the individuals from entering the United States.

[25]22 C.F.R. pt. 41, subpt. J (2012). A visa is not required for H-2A workers coming from Jamaica and certain other Caribbean countries. 8 C.F.R. § 212.1(b) (2012). In these cases, the worker may go directly to a designated port of entry and apply for admission. According to DHS officials, DHS and State are in the process of drafting regulations to end this exemption from the visa requirement, which had its origin several decades ago, and was never revised. Canadian citizens are also visa exempt.

[26]The term "post" refers to a U.S. consulate or embassy abroad.

an applicant's status as illegal entrant or immigration violator, among other reasons.[27]

After receiving the H-2A visa, a worker may present himself at a port of entry to apply for admission into the United States. Upon arrival, DHS's Customs and Border Protection officers verify the worker's eligibility for admission and determine the specific length of stay. Generally, DHS grants the H-2A worker admission for a period of time authorized on the temporary labor certification.

Recent Legislative Proposals to Change the H-2A Program

Several bills were introduced in 2011 to expand use of an electronic system to verify workers' employment eligibility that, if passed, could reduce the availability of undocumented workers and increase the use of the H-2A program. Some of the federal legislative proposals would expand the use of an electronic employment authorization system known as E-Verify, which is currently operated by DHS and the Social Security Administration.[28] A number of states have enacted laws mandating that some or all employers within their state use E-Verify for new hires. Some agricultural employer associations have raised concerns that requiring the use of E-Verify could cause agricultural employers to lose many of their workers. Such a labor shortage could result in more applications for foreign workers through the H-2A program.

Other legislative proposals introduced in 2011 would modify or replace the H-2A program. Congress has considered making changes to the H-2A program as part a larger effort to address immigration issues. Specifically, a legislative proposal known as the Agricultural Job Opportunities, Benefits, and Security Act—or AgJOBS—is said to represent a compromise between major stakeholders and includes provisions to change the H-2A program and develop a new program to legalize the status of undocumented farm workers through a two-stage process. AgJOBS has been introduced several times and was introduced in the Senate as part of the Comprehensive Immigration Reform Act of

---

[27]8 U.S.C. § 1182(a)(2), (3) and (6) and 22 C.F.R. § 21.121 (2012).

[28]E-Verify is an internet-based system intended to electronically verify U.S. work eligibility. For more information, see GAO, *Employment Verification: Federal Agencies Have Taken Steps to Improve E-Verify, but Significant Challenges Remain*, GAO-11-146 (Washington, D.C.: Dec. 17, 2010).

2011 on June 22, 2011.[29] Three other proposed bills would add a role for the U.S. Department of Agriculture in administering the program. Another proposal would, among other things, change the application filing deadline for employers from 45 days to 30 days prior to the date of need and deem any application approved if Labor fails to make a decision within 30 days of the employer's filing date. Other proposals include provisions that would allow employers to hire H-2A workers as dairy workers or livestock herders without being required to show that such positions are of a temporary or seasonal nature.

Employers Cited Challenges with the Largely Paper-Based Process, Implementation of New Rules and Procedures, and Complexity

Most Applications are Approved, but Some Employers Experience Processing Delays

In fiscal year 2011, most employers' applications for H-2A workers were approved, but some employers experienced delays in having their applications for H-2A workers processed. Labor approved 94 percent of the H-2A applications for foreign agricultural workers and processed 63 percent of approved applications by the statutory deadline of at least 30

---

[29]Comprehensive Immigration Reform Act of 2011, S. 1258, 112th Cong. tit. I, pt. V (2011).

days prior to the date workers were to begin work.[30] However, Labor did not process 37 percent of applications by the deadline, including 7 percent of applications approved less than 15 days before workers were needed, leaving little time for employers to petition DHS and for workers to obtain visas from State. According to Labor officials, employers' failure to provide required documentation, such as an approved housing inspection, contributes to processing delays. DHS approved 98 percent of the employer petitions for H-2A workers in fiscal year 2011, and about 72 percent of these petitions were processed within 7 days. However, 28 percent took longer and DHS took a month or longer to process 6 percent of the petitions (see fig. 2). An official at DHS told us that employers have up to 84 days plus the applicable mailing time to provide additional documentation requested by the agency, which can significantly affect how long it takes the agency to process a petition.

---

[30]Our analysis of Labor's timeliness excluded emergency cases, which are applications filed less than 45 days prior to the employer's date of need. We calculated the number of calendar days prior to the certified start date that determinations were made. Labor reported that 85 percent of its determinations were timely in fiscal year 2011. Labor changed the method it uses to calculate timeliness in fiscal year 2011 after the agency began allowing employers additional time (up to 5 days) to submit the documentation required to receive a certification. Labor's method for calculating timeliness allows cases that receive deficiency notices—63 percent of cases in fiscal year 2011—an additional 5 days to submit documentation and considers these cases timely as long as the agency made a determination at least 24 days prior to the date of need (5 days past the deadline). This 5 day extension comes at the expense of processing time available for DHS and State in advance of the date of need because DHS cannot initiate its process in advance of Labor's certification.

Figure 2: H-2A Application Processing Times, Fiscal Year 2011

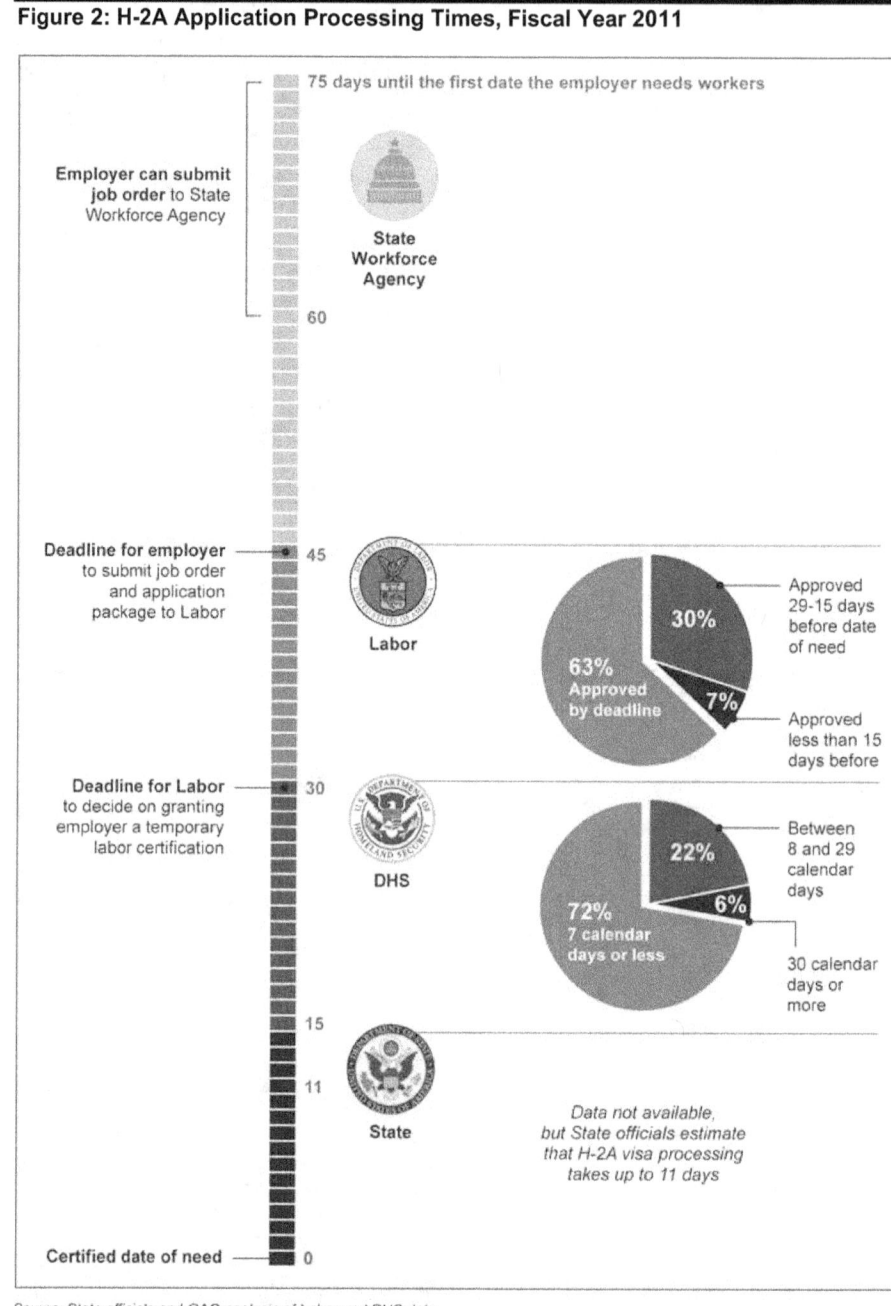

Source: State officials and GAO analysis of Labor and DHS data.

State does not monitor visa processing wait times specifically for H-2A visas, but some employers and State officials we interviewed said delays can occur when large groups of workers apply for visas at peak times during the year at the Monterrey consulate in Mexico, which processes a large proportion of all H-2A visas. State issued visas to 94 percent of the potential H-2A workers who requested them in fiscal year 2011, but it does not collect information on how long it takes posts to process them. Individual posts report estimates of typical wait times for interview appointments and processing of visas in general, but State does not collect data from posts on the amount of time it takes them to process H-2A visas.

H-2A visa processing is concentrated in Mexico. According to data reported by State, in fiscal year 2011, 94 percent of all H-2A visas for workers from all countries worldwide were issued in Mexico and about half were processed by the consulate in Monterrey (see fig. 3). Based on staff estimates, State officials told us that during the peak season at its Monterrey consulate it may take up to 11 days from the time the workers' appointments for finger printing are scheduled until their visas are available for pick up at the consulate.[31] These times can be much shorter at posts that are less busy or during periods that are less busy, according to officials with whom we spoke.

---

[31]After filling out an application, workers must complete a two-part process to obtain an H-2A visa. According to agency officials, first, they visit an Applicant Service Center where they are photographed and fingerprinted. Next, they visit a consulate or embassy where they are interviewed by a Consular Officer during a second appointment on a separate day.

Figure 3: Percent of Worldwide H-2A Visa Applications Processed by Posts in Mexico, Fiscal Year 2011

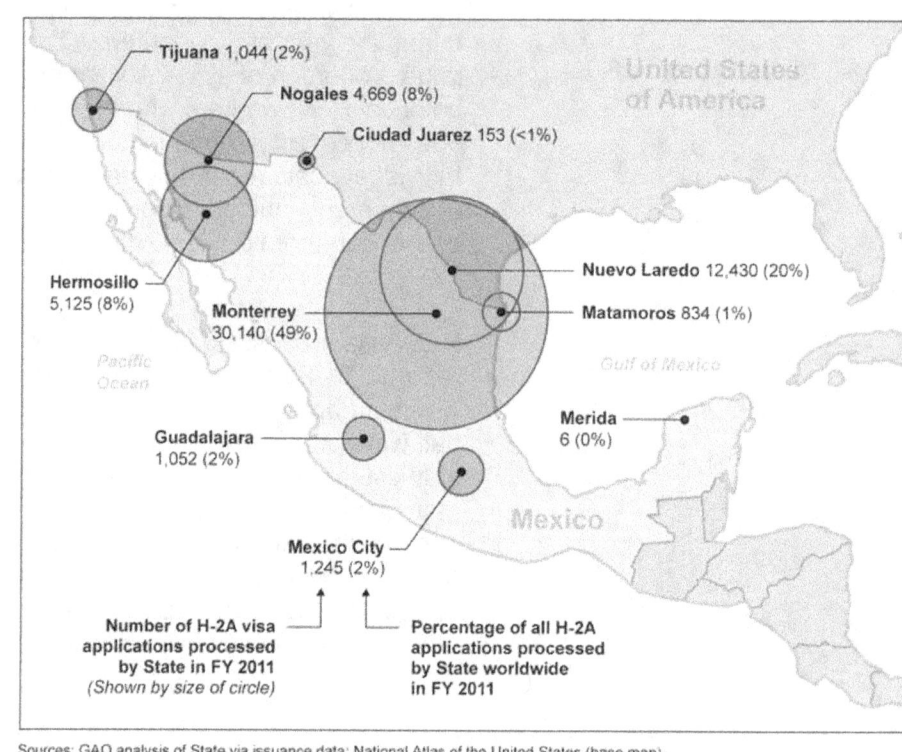

Sources: GAO analysis of State via issuance data; National Atlas of the United States (base map).

Although Labor and DHS have data on their respective application processing times, Labor, DHS, and State lack an integrated system for tracking the applications from the beginning of the process through visa approval. Moreover, they do not collect data to determine the extent to which employers obtain workers by the time they are needed, and the agencies cannot document the total processing time required to complete the H-2A application process. The agencies involved in the H-2A application process largely perform their steps independently and measure their progress independently, in part because none of them has clear authority or responsibility to assess the performance of the process as a whole in achieving timely results for employers, toward which they each contribute. Nor are the agencies expressly required to coordinate their efforts to process applications for H-2A workers. When asked about whether a study could be conducted to determine whether H-2A workers arrive by the employer's date of need, officials from DHS said they are unable to track this information and State officials indicated that this would be beyond the scope of their responsibility. They also said conducting such a study would be difficult because it would involve matching data from multiple agency data systems and could be costly. Each agency has its own strategic plan and performance measures, but none has examined the performance of the H-2A process as a whole. Although the agencies lack data on the reasons for processing delays, our internal control standards suggest agencies monitor critical operating data to support program improvement efforts.[32]

While the agencies do not collect information on the extent to which workers arrive by the date employers state that they are needed, a few employers told us that their workers did not arrive on time. In addition, while not all employers identified delays, about 260 employers who participated in the program in 2010 told the National Council of Agricultural Employers that their H-2A workers began work after the start date they requested on their applications.[33] Seven employers told us that, in the past year, their workers arrived late. For example, one apple grower told us that due in part to processing delays at Labor and DHS in 2010, more than 30 workers arrived 5 days late, resulting in a loss of 15 thousand bushels of apples. Another employer in New York told us that his workers arrived nearly 3 months late, resulting in a loss of about $200,000 worth of unpicked apples, due in part to processing delays at Labor and DHS. Moreover, employers frequently expect delays in the application process according to representatives of four employer associations. A representative for an employer association in North Carolina told us that his members have come to expect that workers will arrive a week late on average. However, in part due to the lack of integrated data, the extent to which these delays can be attributed to employers or specific agencies is unknown.

Inadequate Use of Technology Contributes to Delays

Several employers and agency officials told us that reliance on paper handling can contribute to delays. While State has an online application process that workers can use to apply for a visa, most of the employer's portion of the H-2A application process requires paper handling.

---

[32]GAO, *Internal Control Management and Evaluation Tool,* GAO-01-1008G (Washington, D.C.: August, 2001).

[33]See National Council of Agricultural Employers, H-2A Temporary Agricultural Employee Program (Vienna, V.A.: Nov., 2011).

Specifically, employers must submit paper applications and paper copies of supporting documentation to state workforce agencies, Labor, and DHS (see fig. 4). If the state workforce agency, Labor, or DHS require additional information from employers, they often mail their requests to employers rather than using e-mail. Employers then mail their responses back to the agencies. This system may result in a lengthy back-and-forth process. For example, one employer told us that responding to Labor's deficiency notices—notices explaining why an application cannot be accepted and what corrections needed to be made—sometimes involves using a pen to strike whole paragraphs on the original application and then mailing the entire application back to Labor using overnight mail. Another employer told us that his workers arrived late by the time he responded to multiple inquiries from Labor and DHS.

Figure 4: The Paper-based H-2A Application Process

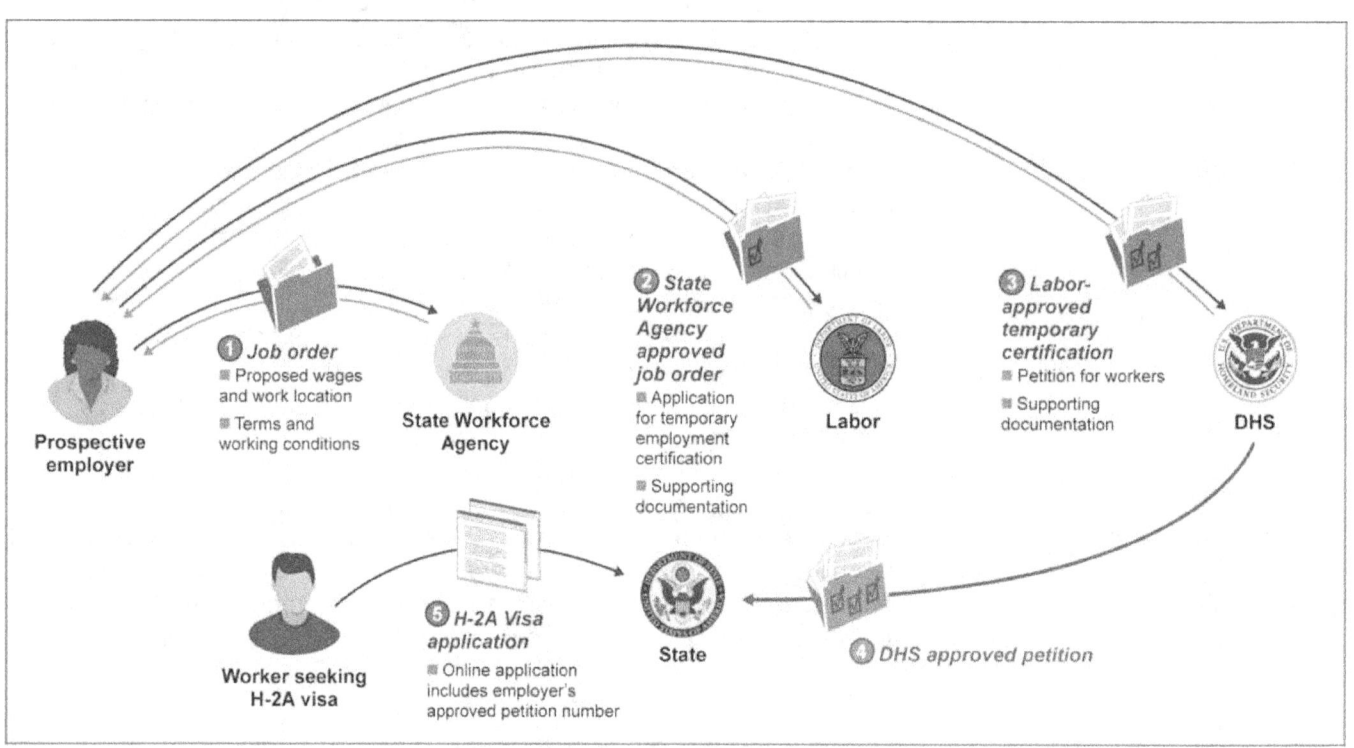

Source: GAO analysis of agency procedures.

Some employers told us that this largely paper-based system can result in lost documentation, delays in communicating with employers, and missed opportunities to quickly resolve minor issues. For example, one employer told us that he experienced delays in 2010 when he mailed his Labor-approved temporary employment certification to DHS, but the agency did not receive it. When the employer called Labor and asked for a replacement, Labor officials told him that they could not send him another one because they do not issue duplicate certifications to employers in order to prevent fraud. After some delay, the employer was able to have DHS request the required documentation from Labor. Similarly, another employer told us that he had to resubmit his paperwork and pay an additional fee when his temporary employment certification was misplaced by DHS's processing center. Officials at DHS also told us that paper handling errors, such as not correctly entering employer responses to agency requests for additional documentation, sometimes result in delays in application processing and that moving to an electronic system could help resolve these issues.[34] Relying less on paper may improve the customer experience for employers using this program. Federal requirements encourage agencies to take specific steps to be results-oriented and customer focused. For example, the Government Performance and Results Act establishes that agencies should develop strategic plans to measure the performance and results of their activities and the President has issued an executive order to improve the quality of service to the public and meet expectations for modern customer service through better use of technology.[35]

Representatives from all of the employer associations we spoke to told us that they had problems communicating with Labor. For example, some employers told us that they did not receive any communication from Labor after submitting their applications until they were mailed deficiency notices telling them that the application could not be accepted. Labor officials told us that, in the past, they would call employers to resolve minor problems or errors, but they now send paper copies of all deficiency notices to employers by mail to better document the process

---

[34] We previously identified inefficiencies with DHS's paper-based processes. DHS agreed with our recommendation to improve the use of technology. See GAO, *Immigration Benefits: Additional Efforts Needed to Help Ensure Alien Files Are Located when Needed*, GAO-07-85 (Washington, D.C.: Oct. 27, 2006); *Information Technology: Near-Term Effort to Automate Paper-Based Immigration Files Needs Planning Improvements*, GAO- 06-375 (Washington, D.C.: Mar. 31, 2006); and *Immigration Benefits: Improvements Needed to Address Backlogs and Ensure Quality of Adjudications*, GAO-06-20 (Washington, D.C.: Nov. 21, 2005).

[35] 5 U.S.C. § 306 and Exec. Order No. 13,571.

and use e-mail to resolve minor deficiencies when possible.[36] In addition, Labor officials said that, due to limited resources, they do not have the capacity to dedicate staff to answering phone calls and that their analysts focus on processing applications rather than responding to inquires from employers. They also noted that they use helpdesk e-mail boxes to provide employers and their representatives with an opportunity to communicate with the agency. In addition, they said the H-2A application fees paid by employers to defray processing costs cannot be used for ongoing administration of the program.[37]

Communication between agencies is also primarily done through paper notifications. The agencies do not communicate their decisions to one another electronically because they lack data sharing capabilities. Specifically, Labor does not communicate with DHS when the agency approves an employer's request for H-2A workers. By regulation, employers are required to provide the original temporary employment certification approved by Labor to DHS, rather than Labor sending it to DHS directly.[38] Officials at DHS told us that the two agencies would need a memorandum of agreement to allow DHS staff to access Labor's system in order to obtain information electronically about the employer's labor certification. Furthermore, although DHS forwards its petition approvals directly to State, the agency does not e-mail the documents to State because, according to agency officials, the two agencies lack mutual encryption technology to protect personally identifiable information. Instead, State must scan the approved petition and supporting documentation in order to adjudicate and process visas for workers. According to State officials, it takes 2 days to scan most employers' petition approval notices after receiving them from DHS.

In addition, employers who need workers at different times of the season must repeat all of the steps of the application process for each group of workers needed within a single season, regardless of whether the same

---

[36]Labor is required by statute to issue a deficiency notice, when applicable, within seven days, ensuring that an employer or its representative receives information about an application within 7 days. 29 U.S.C. § 1188(c)(2).

[37]Revenues generated from H-2A application fees are deposited and combined with other revenue in the General Fund of the U.S. Treasury. The Immigration and Nationality Act provides no mechanism for dedicated use of these funds by the Secretary of Labor.

[38]8 C.F.R. § 214.2(h)(5)(i)(A) (2012).

tasks are involved. Some employers need to stagger the arrival of workers at different points of the harvest season, so that they have the greatest number of workers when the workload is heaviest. Currently, in order to have workers arrive at different points of the season, employers must repeat each step of the application process and file full, separate applications for each additional set of workers, even when the applications are substantially similar and the only difference is the date they indicate workers are needed. According to a representative of an employer association, this can be unnecessarily burdensome because it can be paper-intensive and costly. According to Labor officials, the reason employers need to submit multiple applications is that Labor needs to establish that there is a shortage of U.S. workers each time agricultural employers request foreign workers by reviewing the employer's documentation of recruitment efforts. However, it is less clear why other parts of the application would require resubmission when changes are not required. Some employers we spoke to told us they would prefer being able to file one application and list several different start dates instead of having to resubmit the full application separately for each group of workers, especially if they need workers to arrive within a few weeks of each other, when labor market conditions are unlikely to change substantially.

Implementation of New Rules and Procedures Lengthen Agencies' Processing Times

Employers also reported encountering delays due to increased scrutiny from DHS and Labor after the agencies implemented new rules and procedures in 2008 and 2010, respectively, intended to increase program integrity and worker protection. Labor's H-2A regulations remained largely unchanged from 1987 until 2008, when Labor issued new regulations allowing employers to attest that they met the regulatory requirements of the program, such as providing workers adequate housing, rather than requiring them to submit documentation to demonstrate compliance.[39] Labor later determined that the 2008 regulations did not sufficiently protect workers and issued new regulations in 2010 that reinstated many of the 1987 regulations, including requiring employers to submit documents with their applications to demonstrate compliance.[40] Labor officials told us that the recent regulatory changes resulted in an increased number of deficiency notices while employers adjusted to the

---

[39]52 Fed. Reg. 20,496 (June 1, 1987) and 73 Fed. Reg. 77,110 (Dec. 18, 2008).

[40]75 Fed. Reg. 6,884 (Feb. 12, 2010).

changes. For example, the percentage of employer applications for which Labor issued deficiency notices increased from 7 percent in fiscal year 2006 to 63 percent in fiscal year 2011 (see fig. 5). Labor officials told us their case management system does not currently have the ability to aggregate the reasons for deficiency notices, but that they can identify the reasons on a case-by-case basis. Labor officials also told us that many of these notices were issued because employers used the wrong forms or failed to provide the required documentation in a timely manner.

Figure 5: Percentage of Employer Applications Issued Deficiency Notices from Labor, Fiscal Year 2006-2011

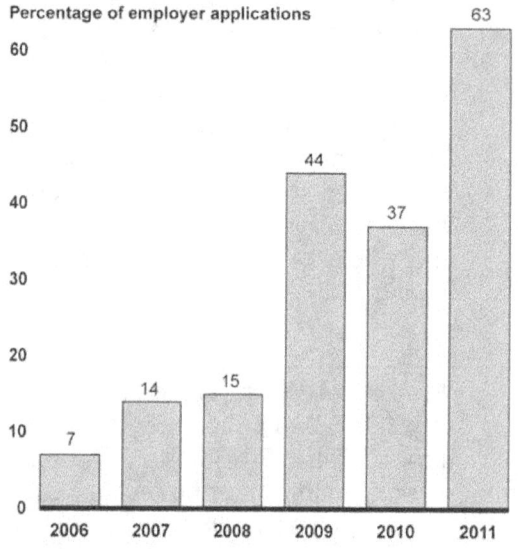

Source: GAO analysis of Department of Labor data.

Many employers said Labor's implementation of these new regulations has made the application process more difficult, resulting in delays and costly appeals. In 2011, Labor issued denials or deficiency letters to employers for various reasons, such as failing to establish a seasonal or temporary need for workers, job requirements that were not consistent with "normal and accepted" practices, and failing to provide a written recruitment report. In addition, employer appeals increased from 15 to 441 from fiscal year 2006 to fiscal year 2011(see fig. 6). Judges dismissed or sent most appeals back to Labor for further processing. Based on Labor's characterization of the 2011 rulings, we counted 72 appeals that resulted in substantive rulings in fiscal year 2011, roughly equally divided between cases that affirmed Labor's decision (38 cases) and others that reversed or partially affirmed it. For example, 19 (26 percent) reversed Labor on the basis that the employer submitted the appropriate evidence, the employer was not given enough time to submit evidence, or the certifying officer misinterpreted Labor's regulations, among other reasons.[41] Appealing denials may be costly and time consuming because employers may need to hire a specialized lawyer to represent them at an administrative hearing according to representatives of two employer associations with whom we spoke. According to Labor officials, most of these appeals resulted from employers not providing required documentation along with their H-2A applications. At the same time, Labor officials said they initially applied a "plain and strict" interpretation of the rules, denying applications for which employers did not provide the required documentation within the statutory deadline for agency processing. The officials added that most applications were approved within a few days of the appeal because employers submitted the required information, but they agreed that the resulting increased rate of denials contributed to an increase in the number of appeals, creating additional burden and delays.

Figure 6: Number of Employer Appeals of Labor's Deficiency Notices/Denials, Fiscal Year 2006-2011

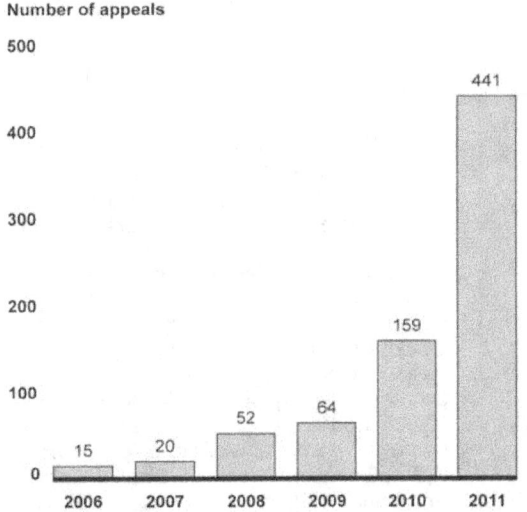

Number of appeals

Source: GAO analysis of decisions made by Labor's Office of Administrative Law Judges.

[41]The rest of the appealed cases that resulted in rulings were mixed rulings and were partially affirmed and partially reversed (15 cases).

GAO-12-706 H-2A Application Process

Some employers experienced delays in obtaining H-2A workers caused by application of new procedures. For example, DHS began using a database that did not have records on some employers who had previously used the H-2A program. Some of these employers experienced delays when DHS began issuing requests for evidence asking for more information, such as tax records, when the employers were not found in the database.[42] Some employers also told us they experienced delays in obtaining H-2A workers from Jamaica because DHS issued requests to employers for evidence about a longstanding practice in which, on behalf of a Jamaican governmental organization, amounts were deducted from the workers' paychecks to fund a health care plan and personal savings accounts.[43] Data from DHS show that although relatively few applications received requests for further evidence, this number has fluctuated in recent years (see fig.7). However, DHS's case management system does not track the reasons for these requests for evidence.

---

[42]To enhance the integrity of the program, DHS began using a web-based database called Validation Instrument for Business Enterprises (VIBE) in 2010 to validate information provided on employers' petitions for H-2A workers.

[43]Employers were asked to provide documentation, such as workers' recent pay stubs, to show that fees are not being deducted from workers' paychecks. DHS and Labor regulations prohibit the collection of fees from workers' paychecks as a condition of H-2A employment. 8 U.S.C. § 214.2(h)(5)(xi) and 20 C.F.R. § 655.20(o) and (p)(2012). The basis for these requests for evidence was to ensure that the practices of the Jamaican governmental organization did not violate the regulatory bans on payment of prohibited fees by workers, which is an essential worker protection against abuse and unfair treatment, according to DHS officials. DHS has posted guidance on prohibited fees on its H-2 web page and conducted national outreach to employers on this topic in June 2011. According to agency officials, specific guidance pertaining to the Jamaican governmental organization has not been issued and these cases are handled the same as other cases involving deductions from workers' paychecks. According to DHS officials, no petitions have been denied recently due to prohibited fees and the number of requests for evidence on this issue has decreased. Labor is currently investigating some employers who use Jamaican workers and officials told us the agency will be publishing general guidance clarifying the permissibility of workers voluntarily requesting deductions from wages under the H-2A program.

Figure 7: Percentage of Employer Applications Receiving Requests for Evidence from DHS, Fiscal Year 2006-2011

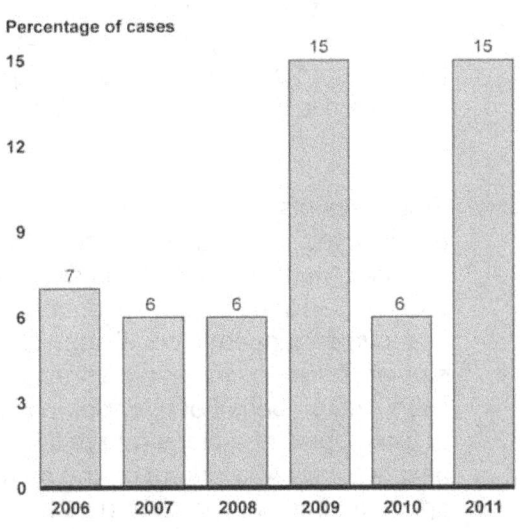

Source: GAO analysis of DHS data

Complexity of the H-2A Program Poses Challenges for Some Employers

Several employers also found some of the program rules and paperwork requirements to be complicated and were confused about the requirements of the H-2A program because some of Labor's decisions seemed inconsistent. Six of the employer representatives we interviewed cited program complexity as a challenge. The H-2A program involves multiple agencies and numerous detailed program rules that sometimes conflict with other laws. For example, because of confusion regarding the H-2A regulations, one employer expressed uncertainty about the appropriate time to reimburse workers for their in-bound travel costs, payment of which must be included in the job offer. The H-2A regulations specify that workers must be reimbursed upon the completion of 50 percent of their work contract but also that H-2A employers may be subject to the Fair Labor Standards Act,[44] under which employers are to make such reimbursements during the first week of employment.[45]

---

[44]20 C.F.R. §§ 655.122(h)(1) and 655.135(e) (2012). Also see Michael Prasad, *We Need Your Help! But It's Gonna Cost You: Arriaga, Castellanos-Contreras, and Why Point of Hire Fees Should be Paid by the Employer,* 33 W. New Eng. L. Rev. 817 (2011).

[45]Employment Standards Administration, Field Assistance Bulletin No. 2009-2 (Aug. 21, 2009).

Another representative of an employer association told us that employers have difficulty knowing how much to pay workers.[46] An employer representative in New York told us that his association advises employers to use a contracting service or an attorney if they are considering using the H-2A program because the program is so complex and difficult to navigate. He noted that some small farmers don't have the resources to hire an attorney or contractor to help them fill out the paperwork.

Employers also frequently reported that they did not understand the H-2A program requirements because Labor's decisions seemed to be inconsistent. Representatives of seven employer associations told us Labor's decisions on the acceptability of the terms and conditions of employment appear inconsistent from year to year or from employer to employer. For example, a contractor told us that an application she submitted on behalf of a farmer in New York was approved for 10 workers to pick apples at a piece rate of 85 cents in March 2011. However, her next order for 45 workers on the same farm the following month was not approved and she was instructed to pay $1 per bushel instead. One Washington employer was allowed to include minimum requirements for how much fruit to pick per day in a 2010 job order but was not allowed to do so in 2011. Another grower in Washington reported being allowed to include a termination clause in a job order while a fellow grower in the same state doing the same type of work was not allowed to include this information, even though the two growers applied for H-2A workers in the same year. In Massachusetts, apple growers were allowed to include experience requirements on their applications after appealing Labor's initial decision prohibiting them from doing so, but vegetable growers were not.[47]

---

[46]Labor's H-2A regulations at 20 CFR 655.120(l) provide that employers must pay their H-2A workers and workers at least the highest of: (i) the Adverse Effect Wage Rate—the minimum wage rate Labor has determined must be offered and paid by employers to H-2A workers so that the wages of similarly employed U.S. workers will not be adversely affected; (ii) the prevailing wage; (iii) the prevailing piece rate; (iv) the agreed-upon collective bargaining wage, if applicable; or (v) the Federal or State minimum wage, in effect at the time the work is performed.

[47]In addition to rulings from previous appeals, the judge found corroborating evidence that apple farming was a difficult and skilled job that required training and knowledge of safety issues. He did not find similar support for vegetable and tobacco farmers. See *Westward Orchards*, 2011-TLC-00411, and *Volante Farms*, 2011-TLC-00412

Agencies Took Steps to Improve the Process, but Delays in Modernization and Unclear Guidance Continue to Pose Challenges

Labor and DHS Efforts to Modernize the Application Process Have Been Delayed

To process applications more efficiently and provide better customer service, Labor and DHS have taken steps to create new electronic applications that will allow employers to file for H-2A workers online, but development and implementation of both applications has been delayed (see table 2).

Table 2: Status of Agency Plans to Deliver Online H-2A Applications, Including Original and Current Planned Implementation Dates

Agency	Originally planned implementation date	Design complete?	Schedule in place for development and implementation?	Current planned implementation date
Labor	August 2011	Yes	Yes	By the end of 2012
DHS	October 2012	No	No	Agency is in the process of developing a schedule

Source: GAO analysis of documents received from Labor and DHS.

Federal law and executive orders provide that federal agencies are to be customer service-focused and executive orders provide that federal agencies use technology to improve the customer experience.[48] Accordingly, in fiscal year 2009, Labor implemented a web-based system for two of its other labor certification programs that allows employers to file applications online and for the agency to process them electronically. Labor is currently in the process of developing an online H-2A application to add to its existing web-based filing system, but it has been delayed.

Specifically, in October 2010, Labor began designing an online H-2A application for employers that it planned to deploy in August 2011.

---

[48]GPRA Modernization Act of 2010, Pub. L. No. 111–352; Exec. Order No. 12,862 (Sept. 11, 1993); Exec. Order No. 13,571 (Apr. 27, 2011).

However, Labor officials told us the online application was delayed because the agency could not award the contract to develop it while operating under a provisional budget based on a continuing resolution. Since then, Labor completed the design of the online H-2A application and in June 2012 awarded the contract to develop, test, and implement it. Labor officials told us they anticipate the online H-2A application will be available for use by employers by the end of 2012 and, according to the development contract, the online application should be available to employers on November 15, 2012. According to Labor officials, the online application will allow employers to create account profiles and check the status of their H-2A applications. In addition, Labor officials said the online H-2A application would also result in faster application processing, reduced costs, better customer service, and improved data quality.

DHS also plans to implement an online petition for H-2A workers, but the agency has experienced delays and is in the process of developing a schedule for completing this work. The agency planned to deploy an online H-2A petition in October 2012 as part of its Transformation Program, which aims to replace the paper-based systems currently used to process petitions with an electronic system. However, the Transformation Program itself has been delayed several times since its inception in 2005, as we have previously reported, and officials told us they have not started work on the online H-2A petition and do not know when it will be completed. In prior work on the Transformation Program, we found DHS was managing the program without specific acquisition management controls, such as reliable schedules, which contributed to missed milestones.[49] DHS officials said they were addressing this report's recommendations and are in the process of developing an integrated master schedule for all Transformation activities, including the online H-2A petition, in accordance with GAO best practices outlined in the report. Once the online petition for H-2A workers is available, employers will be able to file all required documents electronically to petition for H-2A workers, create account profiles, and check the status of their applications. In addition, the agency could streamline benefits processing by eliminating redundant data entry and reducing the number of required forms.

---

[49]GAO, *Immigration Benefits: Consistent Adherence to DHS's Acquisition Policy Could Help Improve Transformation Program Outcomes*, GAO-12-66 (Washington, D.C.: Nov. 22, 2011).

Federal Agencies Updated Processes and Reached Out to Employers, but Labor's Guidance to States Needs Improvement

Recently and over the course of our review, in addition to taking steps to modernize the H-2A application process, federal agencies have taken a number of other steps to improve employers' experience with the application process. Specifically, Labor made changes to its review process to informally resolve issues with employers and reduce unnecessary delays and appeals. Labor officials told us that, in 2011, they piloted using e-mail to communicate with employers in 10 states about their H-2A applications. In March 2012, Labor began using e-mail to communicate with employers in all states about their applications. Labor also changed its procedures so that it can make corrections to minor errors on an employer's H-2A application—such as adding a missing phone number—after obtaining the employer's permission via e-mail to correct the error. In February 2011, Labor instituted a policy that gives employers up to 5 additional days to submit required documentation on their H-2A applications rather than automatically denying them because all of the required documentation was not submitted by the deadline.[50]

In addition to the changes outlined above, since implementing its new regulations in March 2010, Labor provided employers with more guidance about the requirements of the H-2A program in a variety of formats (see table 3).

Table 3: Examples of Labor's Efforts to Provide Additional Guidance to Employers on H-2A Program Requirements, 2010 to 2012

Date released	Description
March 2010 to February 2012	Issued six rounds of answers to frequently asked questions
September 2011 and May 2012	Posted a document with tips on filing an H-2A application on its Web site
October 2011	Developed a new Web site dedicated to the H-2A program, with program updates and materials
December 2011	Published an H-2A Employer guide on its Web site
December 2011 and January 2012	Held webinars about the new March 2010 H-2A rules and interpretations
February 2012	Labor officials attended and presented at conferences attended by H-2A employers
March 2012	Created an H-2A Ombudsman Program office to help employers resolve issues

Source: GAO analysis of Labor documents.

---

[50]20 C.F.R. § 655.130(b) (2012). By statute, Labor is not permitted to require employers to submit their applications more than 45 days before the first date the labor or services of the H-2A worker is required. 8 U.S.C. § 1188(c)(1).

Labor officials said these efforts resulted in improved timeliness and fewer appeals in recent months. Our analysis of Labor's data showed that the agency's timeliness remained relatively unchanged, although the percentage of applications for which deficiency notices were issued and the number of appealed decisions declined substantially over that period. For the first half of fiscal year 2012, Labor processed 61 percent of certified applications at least 30 days prior to the employer's date of need and issued deficiency notices for 38 percent of employer applications. [51] Sixty employer appeals were filed during the first half of fiscal year 2012.

Several employers we interviewed reported that they did not understand the H-2A program requirements because Labor's decisions seemed inconsistent. A number of the inconsistencies employers cited concerned job order terms and conditions, the acceptability of which varies by state. Labor officials told us they strive for consistency and have many checks in place to ensure consistent decisions. Specifically, they said analysts in Labor's processing center follow detailed standard operating procedures and the center has multiple quality assurance methods to ensure consistency, including supervisory review, peer review, and a quarterly quality assurance process. In addition, according to Labor officials, processing center analysts are given an overview of the H-2A program, study the regulations and standard operating procedures, and shadow a more seasoned employee before receiving their own cases to adjudicate. [52] There are also periodic training classes that address adjudication issues that have arisen during the last calendar year.

Labor regulations require H-2A employers to include only terms and conditions that meet or exceed prevailing, normal, or accepted practices, as determined by the state workforce agency. Labor's regulations and its guidance to states allow states to apply different standards to determine whether various terms and conditions are acceptable. [53] For example,

---

[51]The first half of fiscal year 2012 refers to the period October 1, 2011 to March 31, 2012. Results for the entire year may differ.

[52]Our internal control standards state that agency managers should identify the knowledge and skills needed for various jobs and provide necessary training, among other things. GAO, *Standards for Internal Control in the Federal Government*, GAO/AIMD-00.21.3.1 (Washington, D.C.: Nov. 1999).

[53]The most recent comprehensive guidance to states about the H-2A program is Labor's 1988 H-2A Program Handbook. U.S. Department of Labor, Employment and Training Administration, *H-2A Program Handbook*, Handbook No. 398 (Washington, D.C.: January 1988).

GAO-12-706 H-2A Application Process

state workforce agencies are directed to apply a prevailing practice standard to determine whether the frequency with which an employer intends to pay H-2A workers is acceptable, while states can use a more subjective normal and common practice standard to determine whether job qualifications, such as how much experience is required, are acceptable (see table 4).

Table 4: Standards States Use to Determine Acceptable Terms and Conditions in H-2A Job Orders

Applicable standard for approving terms or conditions of employment	Examples of terms and conditions employers address in H-2A job orders to which the standard applies
Prevailing practice: the practice used by half or more of agricultural employers employing a half or more of the workers in the occupation in the area.	• Provision of housing for workers' families • Advancement of required payment for inbound and outbound transportation costs • Frequency of payment
Normal or common practice: Although the terms "normal" and "common" are difficult to quantify, the practice may be less than prevailing, but not unusual or rare. Consistent with what is normally required by non-H-2A employers in the same or comparable occupations and crops in the area.	• Productivity standards (e.g., minimum level of fruit that must be picked to retain employment) • Job qualifications, such as requiring specific experience

Source: U.S. Department of Labor, Employment and Training Administration, H-2A Program Handbook, Handbook No. 398 (Washington, D.C.: January 1988).

In 1988, Labor provided states with an H-2A Program Handbook that included guidance on how to make these decisions and encouraged states to administer formal surveys to determine acceptable practices. If the state workforce agency cannot use a formal survey, Labor's guidance suggests states make these determinations using other information sources, such as staff knowledge and experience, informal surveys, reviews of job orders used by non-H-2A employers, or consultation with experts in agriculture or farm worker advocates. In 2011, Labor began posting results from states' prevailing practice surveys online to help employers write job orders that are consistent with prevailing, normal, and accepted practices.

Labor's guidance to states for determining acceptable practices, however, is broad and not prescriptive, leading states to apply varied methods, some of which may be insufficient. For example, the Administrative Law Judge who ruled on the Massachusetts apple and vegetable growers' appeal of Labor's initial decision to prohibit experience requirements did not consider the Massachusetts state workforce agency's prevailing practice survey in his ruling because of its design flaws. Further, two employer representatives told us they considered state prevailing practice

GAO-12-706 H-2A Application Process

surveys to be unreliable and inconsistent in their coverage. In addition, officials in the three states we visited said they did not include questions about certain terms and conditions in formal surveys and used different methods to determine whether a particular practice was acceptable: two states reviewed job orders filed by non-H-2A employers; the other state informally surveyed non-H-2A employers in-person. One employer representative expressed frustration that neighboring states used different methods to determine acceptable practices for the same crop and that the results differed.

DHS also has taken several steps to improve employers' experience with the H-2A application process. Specifically, the agency took steps to expedite petitions for H-2A workers and provide more guidance to employers. In October 2007, DHS directed its employees to expedite the handling and adjudication of H-2A petitions. According to our analysis, the agency's processing times have improved in recent years. From fiscal year 2006 to fiscal year 2011, the percentage of petitions approved within 1 week increased from about 34 percent to 72 percent. At the same time, the percentage of petitions that took 1 month or longer to approve declined from about 11 percent to about 6 percent. In July 2010 and June 2011, DHS invited employers to participate in teleconferences to discuss employers' difficulties with some of its new systems and procedures. In addition, the agency posted summaries of the teleconferences and answers to employers' frequently asked questions on its Web site.

State has addressed employer concerns with the H-2A visa application process by hosting face-to-face meetings with employers and other key stakeholders, making improvements to its worker processing procedures, and taking steps to increase the capacity of its Monterrey consulate to process H-2A visas. In 2012, State officials said they reached out to Labor to discuss H-2A related issues. They also said the two agencies are formalizing working groups in part to improve information sharing. State also meets with employers and other stakeholders at annual meetings that bring together representatives from Labor, DHS, and State. Officials from Labor and DHS, and State's contractor attended the most recent of these meetings, held in Texas in January 2012. A representative of an employer association who attended this meeting told us it was helpful to have representatives from all three agencies there to answer questions. After hearing at the January 2012 meeting that some employers had difficulties with getting their Mexican H-2A workers processed by their date of need, State directed employers with approaching dates of need to request emergency appointments for their workers to be processed at posts other than the Monterrey consulate.

State officials noted that all Mexican posts have the capacity to process H-2A visa applications and suggested that applicants can visit other posts if it is difficult to get appointments at the Monterrey consulate. State also developed new procedures to better enable them to handle large groups of workers. In addition, State is expanding its Monterrey consulate, which currently handles most of the H-2A visas processed. Officials said the new facility is scheduled to open in 2014, although they were uncertain whether future staffing levels at the facility would increase.

Conclusions

The H-2A program is a means through which agricultural employers can legally hire temporary foreign workers when there is a shortage of U.S. workers. The H-2A application process consists of a series of sequential steps conducted by varied agencies, no one of which bears responsibility for monitoring or assessing the performance of the process as a whole. Negotiating this largely paper-based process can be time consuming, complex, and challenging for employers. The associated difficulties can impose a burden on H-2A employers that is not borne by employers who break the law and hire undocumented workers. Although Labor and DHS have taken some steps to incorporate new technologies, delays in the development of electronic application filing systems continue burdening employers with paperwork and may be consuming more resources from federal agencies than necessary. In addition, the absence of systems to collect data on the reasons for processing delays makes it difficult for these agencies to identify why employer applications are initially rejected, to target their efforts to address the most important issues that challenge employers, and to improve performance. Meanwhile, employers who require workers at different points of the season must bear the additional costs of submitting paperwork to multiple agencies for each set of workers. In addition, employers continue to express confusion about how state workforce agencies and Labor are applying Labor's new regulations. Without additional clarification and transparency, employers may continue to submit unacceptable paperwork that requires extra resources from all parties to process. As immigration rules are tightened and the economy improves for U.S. workers, more employers may need to use the H-2A program to obtain foreign workers. This potential influx of new users could exacerbate existing problems if changes are not made to improve the application process.

Recommendations for Executive Action

To improve the timeliness of application processing, as part of creating new online applications, we recommend that the Secretaries of Labor and Homeland Security:

- develop a method of automatically collecting data on the reasons for deficiency notices, requests for additional evidence, and denials, and use this information to develop strategies to improve the timeliness of H-2A application processing. Such information could help the agencies determine whether, for example, employers may need more guidance or staff may need more training.

To reduce the burden on agricultural employers and improve customer service, we recommend that the Secretary of Labor:

- permit the use of a single application with staggered dates of need for employers who need workers to arrive at different points of a harvest season. Employers could still be required to submit evidence of their recruitment efforts, but would not be required to resubmit a full application for each set of workers needed during the season.

To promote consistency and transparency of decisions made about the acceptability of employer applications and clarify program rules, we recommend that the Secretary of Labor:

- review and revise, as appropriate, guidance provided to state workforce agencies on methods to determine the acceptability of employment practices. This guidance should be made available to employers and published on Labor's Web site.

Agency Comments and Our Evaluation

We provided a draft of this report to Labor, DHS, and State for review and comment. State had no comments. Labor and DHS provided written comments which are reproduced in appendices I and II. Labor and DHS also provided technical comments, which we incorporated as appropriate. DHS concurred with our recommendation that the agency develop a method to automatically collect additional data through its forthcoming electronic application system to improve the timeliness of application processing. Similarly, Labor agreed with our recommendation that the agency develop a method of automatically collecting data on the reasons for deficiency notices and use this information to develop strategies to improve the timeliness of H-2A application processing and noted that it would explore the resources required to collect such information as part of its online application system. Labor also agreed with our recommendation that it update the guidance it provides to state workforce agencies on methods to determine the acceptability of employment practices.

Labor did not agree with our recommendation that it allow employers to file a single application per season for workers arriving on different start dates, stating that the department's regulations define the date of need as the first date the employer requires the services of all H-2A workers that are the subject of the application, not an indication of the first date of need for only some of the workers. Labor stated that having each employer file a single application with staggered dates of need would result in one recruitment for job opportunities that could begin many weeks or months after the original date of need, which could nullify the validity of the required labor market test. We are not recommending that employers conduct a single labor market test corresponding with their earliest date of need. Employers should still be required to submit evidence of their recruitment efforts for every start date listed on each application, but we believe they should not be required to resubmit a full application package for each set of workers needed during a season.

Labor also expressed concern that our report points to the experiences of some employers or those of a single employer to support our conclusions. As noted earlier in this report, information obtained from our interviews cannot be generalized to all states or all agricultural employers. In addition, the illustrations used in this report highlight challenges expressed by numerous employers with whom we spoke, even when we used one employer's experience as an example. Further, as we noted previously, agency data are not available to document the extent of some employer challenges, such as whether workers arrive by the date they are needed by employers.

As agreed with your offices, unless you publicly announce the contents of this report earlier, we plan no further distribution until 7 days from the report date. At that time, we will send copies to the appropriate congressional committees, the Secretaries of Homeland Security, Labor, State, and other interested parties. In addition, this report will be available at no charge on the GAO Web site at http://www.gao.gov.

If you or your staff members have any questions regarding this report, please contact me at (202) 512-7215 or moranr@gao.gov. Contact points for our Offices of Congressional Relations and Public Affairs may be found on the last page of this report. GAO staff who made major contributions to this report are listed in appendix III.

Sincerely yours,

Revae E. Moran

Revae Moran, Director
Education, Workforce
    and Income Security Issues

Appendix I: Comments from the Department of Labor

U.S. Department of Labor

Assistant Secretary for
Employment and Training
Washington. D.C. 20210

AUG 3 1 2012

Ms. Revae Moran,
Director
Education, Workforce, and
Income Security Issues
U.S. Government Accountability Office
441 G. Street, N.W.
Washington, D.C. 20548

Dear Ms. Moran:

We want to thank you for the opportunity to review and comment on the Government Accountability Office's (GAO) draft report entitled, *H-2A Visa Program: Modernization and Improved Guidance Could Reduce Employer Application Burden (GAO-12-706)*.

The Department's H-2A performance data indicate that employers are successfully using the program, and we continue to take steps to help H-2A employers meet their regulatory obligations and to process applications more efficiently. In the past year, the Department initiated a number of actions designed to clarify program requirements for participating employers and improve program performance. The Department engaged in extensive outreach and education efforts to familiarize program users with regulatory changes implemented through the 2010 H-2A Final Rule. The Department continues its efforts to make the program more effective and efficient for employers, including launching a more user friendly H-2A Web site that features a new H-2A Employer Handbook, and posting updated Filing Tips, Frequently Asked Questions, and other technical assistance materials -- all aimed at assisting small growers. The Department continues to meet with employers and other stakeholders to provide additional assistance and explanation of the H-2A program's requirements.

We are pleased that our performance administering the H-2A program has improved significantly over prior years. For Fiscal Year (FY) 2011, the Department certified 93 percent of all H-2A applications filed covering more than 74,000 farm worker positions, with approximately 85 percent of our final decisions issued on time. For the first nine months of FY 2012, the Department has received more than 4,975 H-2A applications requesting more than 75,000 farm workers, a 12 percent increase in applications filed over the same time period in FY 2011. Employers received certifications for approximately 97 percent of all H-2A applications processed, with more than 83 percent of our final decisions issued timely.

However, the Department is aware that the process of issuing deficiency notices to employers may lead to multiple communications, and possibly delay the rendering of a final decision on its H-2A application. In an effort to improve customer service and provide greater assistance to the employer community in complying with program requirements, the Department expanded the use of e-mail to quickly communicate and resolve minor deficiencies with employer-filed H-2A

1

---

applications. Once an employer corrects these minor deficiencies, the application and job order
are accepted for processing, and the employer is provided with instructions for completing the
application process. This H-2A E-Mail Notification Program has been well received by the
grower community and as a result, our deficiency rate has significantly decreased. For the first
nine months of FY 2012, the percent of employer-filed applications requiring a formal notice of
deficiency fell substantially to 36 percent, compared to approximately 63 percent in FY 2011.

At the outset of the implementation of the H-2A 2010 Final Rule, the Department experienced a
significant increase in initial application denials and subsequent appeals compared to prior years.
Based on data collected from case adjudications, the Department determined that one of the most
common reasons for denial is that employers do not provide the documentation required to issue
the labor certification within 30 days of the employer's need – the statutory time period within
which the Department must issue the determination. Those denials often force growers into the
program's appellate process, which creates additional delays. To ameliorate this problem, the
Department, within the limits of its statutory requirements, implemented a more flexible process
in January 2011, to provide employers with additional time to submit documents necessary to
meet program requirements and receive certification rather than a denial. These revised
procedures have significantly reduced the number of appeals filed. For the first nine months of
FY 2012, approximately 79 appeals were filed with the Department's Office of the
Administrative Law Judges, compared to approximately 441 in FY 2011.

With this in mind, the GAO report identified the following three recommendations for the
Department to address:

1. *To improve the timeliness of application processing, as part of creating new online
    applications, we recommend that the Secretaries of Labor and Homeland Security develop a
    method of automatically collecting data on the reasons for deficiency notices, requests for
    additional evidence, and denials, and use this information to develop strategies to improve
    the timeliness of H-2A application processing. Such information could help the agencies
    determine whether, for example, employers may need more guidance or staff may need more
    training.*

    The Department agrees with this recommendation, but at this time it has no automated
    method of collecting data on the reasons for deficiencies, requests for additional evidence,
    and denials. The H-2A on-line filing module within the iCERT Visa Portal System, which is
    scheduled for implementation in December 2012, will not initially collect this specific
    information; however, the Department will explore the level of resources required to include
    this kind of collection and reporting function.

    While the Department has no automated method of collecting and tracking deficiencies, the
    manner in which H-2A applications are processed at its Chicago National Processing Center
    (NPC) allows staff to extract up-to-date information from case files about the reasons for
    deficiencies and denials. Center staff then review and communicate to the filing community
    through (a) posted H-2A Employer Filing Tips to inform employers of common mistakes that
    may result in processing delays; (b) Frequently Asked Questions (FAQs); and (c) an H-2A
    Employer Handbook. These tools, as GAO acknowledges and which are publicly available

2

at http://www.foreignlaborcert.doleta.gov, explain and clarify key regulatory requirements
for a U.S. employer to successfully participate in the H-2A program.

The Department also recently established an H-2A Ombudsman Program, whose primary
purpose is to facilitate the fair and equitable resolution of concerns that arise within the H-2A
program community. It does so by conducting independent and impartial inquiries into
issues related to the administration of the program and proposing internal recommendations
designed to continuously improve the quality of services provided by the OFLC.

2. *To reduce the burden on agricultural employers and improve customer service, we
recommend that the Secretary of Labor permit applicants to use a single application with
staggered dates of need for employers who need workers to arrive at different points of the
harvest season. Employers could still be required to submit evidence of their recruitment
efforts, but would not be required to resubmit the full application for each set of workers
needed during the season.*

An application for Temporary Employment Certification must contain a single date of need
for all workers under that application. Staggering the date of need for some or all workers in
a single application would result in less protection for American workers and hinder the
Department from fulfilling its statutory obligation to ensure that there are no able, willing
and qualified U.S. workers available to perform the work.

The Department's regulations at 20 CFR 655.103 define the date of need as the first date the
employer requires the services of H-2A and U.S workers as indicated in the *Application for
Temporary Employment Certification*. The date is not an indication of the first date of need
for some workers, but for all the workers that are the subject of the application. The filing of
an application indicates that the employer has full-time work available for all positions it is
requesting for that single start date and that all information reflects the employer's true
temporary need. The date of need is a critical element of the H-2A labor certification process
because it also defines the earliest date when recruiting of U.S. workers can begin. In turn,
recruiting of U.S. workers closer to the date of need is critical to an effective test of the labor
market.

Single applications with staggered dates of need would result in one recruitment for job
opportunities that may begin many weeks or months after the original date of need. This
would suppress applications from U.S. workers who are unable or unwilling to commit to
jobs that are distant in time. As a result, changing the date of need for some or all workers
nullifies the validity of the labor market test, which eliminates the Department's basis for
granting the labor certification.

3. *To promote consistency and transparency of decisions made about the acceptability of
employer applications and clarify program rules, we recommend that the Secretary of Labor
review and revise, as appropriate, guidance provided to state workforce agencies on methods
to determine the acceptability of employment practices. This guidance should be made
available to employers and published on Labor's Web site.*

3

The Department agrees that updated guidance to state workforce agencies on methods to determine the acceptability of employment practices would clarify program rules and provide greater transparency of decisions made about the acceptability of employer applications. The Department recognizes that current guidance, while upheld consistently in the Department's administrative decisions, needs revision to reflect current regulatory processes.

Although the purpose of GAO's report was to examine employer challenges with the H-2A application process, the report could better reflect the necessary balance the Department must strike between employer requirements and worker protections. The Department's statutory responsibility is to certify only those applications for which qualified U.S. workers are not available to perform the work and the employment of foreign workers will not adversely affect the wages and working conditions of similarly employed U.S. workers.

Additionally, despite stating on page 3 that "[i]nformation obtained from our site visits and employer interviews cannot be generalized to all states or agricultural employers," the report later relies on the experiences and opinions of "some employers" or, more significantly, a single employer, to support its conclusions. In our view, reliance on a single employer's experiences to draw conclusions about the Department's practices in dealing with all employers, a method that is found throughout the draft report, is not consistent with the Department's and employers' experiences as supported by data.

Enclosed are the Department's additional technical comments on the draft report. If you would like additional information, please do not hesitate to call me at (202) 693-2700.

Sincerely,

Jane Oates
Assistant Secretary

Enclosure

4

Appendix II: Comments from the Department of Homeland Security

U.S. Department of Homeland Security
Washington, DC 20528

**Homeland
Security**

August 28, 2012

Revae Moran, Director
Education, Workforce, and Income Security Issues
U.S. Government Accountability Office
441 G Street, NW
Washington, DC 20548

Re: Draft Report GAO-12-706, "H-2A VISA PROGRAM: Modernization and Improved
   Guidance Could Reduce Employer Application Burden"

Dear Ms. Moran:

Thank you for the opportunity to review and comment on this draft report. The U.S. Department
of Homeland Security (DHS) appreciates the U.S. Government Accountability Office's (GAO's)
work in conducting its review and issuing this report.

The Department is pleased to note GAO's positive acknowledgement of DHS's continued
progress in the approval of H-2A petitions. In particular, we appreciate GAO's recognition that
over 90 percent of employer petitions for H-2A workers were approved in Fiscal Year, (FY)
2011. As of June 2012, over 98 percent had been approved in FY 2012. Petitions not requiring
the issuance of a request for evidence were, on average, processed within 11 days of receipt.
However, for those cases that required a request for evidence in order to reach a final decision,
the processing time increased in correlation to the responsiveness of the petitioner. In order to
reduce the number of requests for evidence needed, DHS will continue gathering information
(using the traditional methods discussed below) on stakeholder issues or concerns and providing
additional guidance for its customers and staff to ensure the efficient processing of employer
petitions for H-2A workers.

The draft report contained one recommendation made to DHS, with which the Department
concurs. Specifically, GAO recommended the Secretaries of Labor and Homeland Security:

Recommendation: Develop a method of automatically collecting data on the reasons for
deficiency notices, requests for additional evidence, and denials, and use this information to
develop strategies to improve the timeliness of H-2A application processing. Such information
could help the agencies determine whether, for example, employers may need more guidance or
staff may need more training.

Response: Concur. U.S. Citizenship and Immigration Services (USCIS) has investigated
possible avenues for implementing this type of electronic reporting. Although USCIS has the

ability to track case action, its systems are currently not configured to identify the reason that
each individual petition is deficient.[1]

Even if USCIS had the ability to track the filing deficiencies, we do not believe this is the only
means of identifying problematic areas of adjudication. USCIS has historically gathered
information directly from other federal agencies (e.g., the Departments of Labor and State), from
the public through outreach sessions, from quality review processes, and in the resolution of
individual petitioner inquiries. These existing methods have enabled USCIS to develop tools to
assist the public and to improve training programs at USCIS Service Centers.

As mentioned in this report, recognizing that delays in adjudications are especially burdensome
for H-2A petitioners, USCIS provided H-2A petitioners with additional information about how
to properly file the Form I-129. *H-2A Petitioners Questions and Answers* and *Form M-797,
Optional Checklist for Form I-129 H-2A Filings*[2] were developed and posted on the USCIS
Website to address the most common filing errors. In addition, USCIS hosted a stakeholder
meeting on June 10, 2011, to discuss best filing practices for H-2A petitions. During the
meeting, USCIS provided clarification on how petitioners seeking H-2A classification should
complete the Form I-129. For more information about what was discussed during the meeting,
see *Executive Summary of the USCIS Stakeholder Engagement, H-2A Agricultural Workers*[3].

USCIS Service Center personnel are under direction to process the H-2A petitions as
expeditiously as possible, see *October 19, 2007 Neufeld memo on the Updated Procedures for
H-2A (agricultural worker) I-129 Petitions*[4]. On the basis of guidance in this memo, USCIS
makes an initial decision to either approve the petition or request additional evidence promptly
after receipt of the H-2A Form I-129. If additional evidence is needed, the petitioners are given
up to 12 weeks to provide the necessary documentation. USCIS cannot make a final decision
until the petitioner has responded to request for evidence.

USCIS analysis of all Form I-129 petitions filed on behalf of H-2A workers received from
January 2011 to June 2012 showed that USCIS approved the majority of H-2A petitions without
the need to issue a Request for Evidence (RFE). In fact, since January 2011, the H-2A
classification has continued to have one of our highest approval rates among all nonimmigrant
employment-based classifications, as the following table indicates.

---

[1] Electronic filing of employment-based visas is currently scheduled for inclusion in the Electronic Immigration
System in FY 2015. They were moved further back in the schedule (from the originally planned date of June 2014)
pursuant to a request from the business owners. The ability to run reports showing the reason for denial or request
for evidence may be in place prior to FY 2015 because it is likely to be prioritized for a preceding form type.
[2] Links to these documents may be found at www.uscis.gov/h-2a
[3] Links to these documents may be found at
http://www.uscis.gov/USCIS/Outreach%20Notes%20from%20Previous%20Engagements/2011/June%202011/H2A_VI
BE_exec_summ.pdf
[4] Links to these documents may be found at
http://connect.uscis.dhs.gov/workingresources/immigrationpolicy/Documents/H2AFieldGdnc101907.pdf

2

Rates of Approvals, Denials, Request for Evidence

	Approvals	Denials	RFEs	Approval Rate	Denial Rate	RFE Rate*
Jan-11	663	36	113	94.8%	5.2%	16.1%
Feb-11	1107	14	142	98.7%	1.3%	12.6%
Mar-11	1028	4	281	99.6%	0.4%	27.2%
Apr-11	815	8	161	99.0%	1.0%	19.6%
May-11	507	9	63	98.3%	1.7%	12.2%
Jun-11	341	5	56	98.6%	1.4%	16.2%
Jul-11	270	9	63	96.8%	3.2%	22.6%
Aug-11	321	6	56	98.2%	1.8%	14.1%
Sep-11	226	7	63	97.0%	3.0%	15.9%
Oct-11	207	4	32	98.1%	1.9%	15.2%
Nov-11	256	5	102	98.1%	1.9%	39.1%
Dec-11	382	8	77	97.9%	2.1%	19.7%
Jan-12	577	8	69	98.6%	1.4%	11.8%
Feb-12	1127	10	146	99.1%	0.9%	12.8%
Mar-12	1265	13	155	99.0%	1.0%	12.1%
Apr-12	802	13	82	98.4%	1.6%	10.1%
May-12	496	7	95	98.6%	1.4%	18.9%
Jun-12	525	8	27	98.5%	1.5%	5.1%
Total	9,145	124	1,528	98.4%	1.6%	17.0%

*Source: USCIS Office of Performance and Quality

Again, thank you for the opportunity to review and comment on this draft report. Technical comments were previously provided under separate cover. Please feel free to contact me if you have any questions. We look forward to working with you in the future.

Sincerely,

Jim H. Crumpacker
Director
Departmental GAO-OIG Liaison Office

3

Appendix III: GAO Contact and Staff Acknowledgments

GAO Contact	Revae Moran, Director, (202) 512-7215 or moranr@gao.gov
Staff Acknowledgments	In addition to the individual named above, Betty Ward-Zukerman, Assistant Director; Hedieh Rahmanou Fusfield, Jeffrey G. Miller, and Cathy Roark made key contributions to this report. Also contributing were Hiwotte Amare, James Bennett, Kathy Leslie, Jonathan McMurray, Jean McSween, Kathleen van Gelder, and Craig Winslow.

www.ingramcontent.com/pod-product-compliance
Lightning Source LLC
Chambersburg PA
CBHW080917290526
45795CB00007BA/2552